<u>LET THE TRUTH BE TOLD:</u>
Life of Women on the Down Low

For ordering, booking, permission, or questions, contact the author.

ISBN 10: 0615414273
ISBN 13: 978-0-615-41427-0

Printed in the United States of America
First Printing 2010

Edited by: HER TRU SOUL PUBLISHING

Illustrations by: Darrell Gilbert email: dgart9201@yahoo.com

CONTENTS

Chapter 7 – Let the Truth Be Told

Chapter 8 – Mother and Child

Chapter 9 – I Just Don't Get It

Chapter 10 – The Male Perspective

Special Thanks

I'm grateful for having the opportunity to have shared time, laughter, hugs, dreams and most of all, my HEART with these amazing women.

You have been inspiring, motivating, encouraging and loving through the years of my growth. THANK YOU!

To the women whom I've shared their stories in this book, and to the women who stories I didn't share. I LOVE YOU!

Introduction

I want to first say "Thank you" for supporting my second project . This book is the TRUTH, the whole TRUTH and nothing but the TRUTH. LET THE TRUTH BE TOLD, EXPLAINS LIFE OF WOMEN ON THE DOWN LOW.
The Church woman, the Bisexual woman, the Bi-curious woman, the Confused woman, the Married woman, the Best Friend, the Real Lesbian woman, the Lesbian parent, the Heterosexual woman and last, but not least, the Male perspective on *women vs. women.*

LET THE TRUTH BE TOLD is raw, graphic and explicit in content. Be prepared and ready to dive right into love, lust and tell all of women on women relationships.

Learn why women gravitate towards other women. Learn if it's just sexual or emotional. Learn why women have been on the down low and will they remain on the down low.

Holier Than Thou
(The Church Woman)

Chapter 1

Holier Than Thou
(The Church Woman)

These women are clearly on the down low. They are so confused with *"If it's so wrong, then why does it feel so right"* attitude. Some of these women were homophobic in the past. Why, you ask, well you know some of us don't like what reflects whom and what we are. These holier than thou women, some even married to Pastors, which makes them a First Lady, loving the touch and sweet smell of a woman. They know the Word inside and out, but justify their feelings of lust, passion, anticipation and even love with "Us meeting is no coincidence". Their thoughts of sex, intimacy and pure bliss overshadow what God says about homosexuality, fornication and even adultery.

Holier Than Thou

(The Church Woman-Angie's Story)

Oh, not one minister, but two. Some would say "Hallelujah", but I would say, "Umm hmmm".

Angie and I were introduced to one another on a cold, icy, snowy day, but by the end of our encounter, we were both feeling just a wee-bit warmer inside.

I was the Barber, she was the client. Week after week, whenever she would come and sit in my chair, I would caress her hair and neck so softly. Her questions became more involved as well as my answers. We talked about whether we were seeing anyone, what interested us and what didn't. By the end of that appointment, I wanted more. I, oh so wasn't ready for it to end. I'm impatient and I couldn't wait another week to smell her. She was wearing maturity, education and independence. I, oh so wanted some of "that". I had lust in my eyes, she saw it too, and that's why she invited me over….

Over for…

Of course, dinner, hot pants.

I arrived a little early because I was anxious, but also a little nervous. She opened the door, introduced me to her two handsome teenage boys. The four of us sat, ate and talked about general subjects. After dinner, I, of course, helped clean up. Then the boys ran off to do what teenage boys do, so that allowed us time to talk more intimately.

I expressed to her early on during our chair side visits that I was a lesbian, and while we were talking, she stated that she had never been with a woman "in an intimate or sexual manner" she's a woman of God, a Licensed Minister. She's never had any gay friends, let alone, knew of any that are out and open like myself.

She said she feels that her purpose in my life is to bring me closer to Jesus. I'm sitting there thinking, "Yeah OK". Her mouth is saying one thing, but that body language is telling me the total opposite.

I continue to listen as she talked more about how she was raised in church, how she had a calling on her life to be saved at the tender age of 11 years old. She raved on about how important she is, how people look up to her and that she can be my friend, but not in a public setting. She states that she can't be linked to a gay woman, (*one that's openly gay anyway*) in public.

The more she expressed her love for God, the more expressive her feelings toward me became.
The more she prayed in church, the more we talked in person.
The more Sunday services she attended, the more she invited me over.
The more she expressed how important her relationship with God was, the more public we became.
The more she expressed how religious her family was, the more family functions I was taken to.
The more she expressed how she didn't tithe the way the church said, the more she took care of me financially.

The more passive I was, the more aggressive she became.
The more she introduced me as her friend, the more I became her lover.
The more she praised and worshiped our heavenly Father, the more screams and moans I got in the bedroom.
The more "Amens" she verbalized,
(*The more "I want and need you"*) she whispered.
The more she greeted and mingled with the church folk, the more we danced around the room naked.

The louder she turned up the Clarke Sisters, the more in tune she became with my body.
The way Angie felt about us publicly bothered me a lot because for one, I haven't dated anyone before that was discreet, but I enjoyed her so much that I complied. Our relationship grew from "I like you", to "I love you", to "I'm in love with you". Our relationship thrived for years on companionship, honesty and family values.
Holier Than Thou

Holier Than Thou

(The Church Woman-Jackie's Story)

Oh. how sweet and untainted she was. The pureness that protrudes through her skin. The innocence she fights so hard to portray on the exterior but that inner freak that isn't talked about in church is tired of being respectful, wholesome and boring. She wants to be excited, caressed, and spellbound into pure romance.

Handled like "**handled**"…
You know. like the movies.
Yes, that's how we eventually ended up in bed tossing and turning I'm on top, then she's leaning over the bed whispering my name

"Shawna"

Our initial meeting was pure business. She was intrigued by my writings, my story, my life, and my past. not knowing that she would become my future. That first visit left us both wanting more of what each other had to offer. We started engaging in conversation that lasted for hours 'til dawn most mornings talking about us, sharing about us, and making plans to unite us. We were joined you could say, just within a short period of time. We would talk all night, text all day, and beholding onto our last visit, not knowing quite when the next one will be. Our conversations were real, true, honest, deep, encouraging, and spiritual. Our texts were breath taking enticing and left you moist by the time you pressed send. I opened up to her emotionally as well as she opened up to me physically.
We were from two separate worlds two totally different backgrounds. She researched, studied, prepared and delivered sermons. I took numbers, gifts, propositions, and meditated on the invitations that were thrown my way from women.

14

Holier Than Thou

The Church Woman

Questions and Answers

How should the church view you and homosexuality?
The church should view me as an equal, a child of God, one that needs guidance, support, assistance and help with building my relationship with God and not worry about what the church folk think. And in reference to how they should view homosexuality they should view it the same way that God views it but not single it out like it's the worse sin of all, which they do. God views homosexuality, idolatry, fornication, adultery, gossiping, drunkards, thieves etc. all the same way, no sin is greater than the next, God doesn't put levels on sin. 1 Cor. 6:9

Does God love me?
Yes. God loves me, God loves the idolater, God loves the fornicator, God loves the adulterer, God loves the gossiper, God loves the drunkard, and God loves the thief. God is love and He is waiting for me as well as the rest of y'all to follow the will that He has on our life.

Does God judge me?
I think He gives us commandments and leaves it up to us to follow or not. He lays down consequences for our actions just like any law enforcement or parent and if you put them both together then what do you have? God.

Were you raised in church?
Yes. I was raised in church.

What was taught about homosexuality?
As a child I don't recall hearing any sermons on homosexuality, as I grew older and felt drawn to women those kinds of sermons always caught my attention. What was taught or impressed upon me is that homosexuality is an abomination, which was confusing to me because growing up my

16

desires felt natural and right.

Could you ever be open with your sexuality in church?
No, I cannot.

What is your greatest pleasure from a woman?
My greatest pleasure is her embrace.

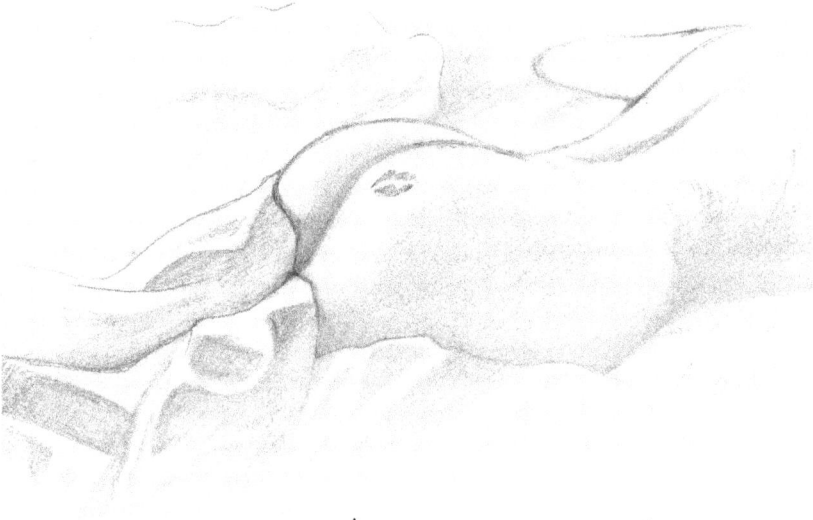

A Lady In The Streets...
But A Freak
In The Sheets
(The Bi-Sexual Woman)

Chapter 2

A Lady in the Street, but a Freak in the Sheets
(The Bi-Sexual Woman)

Now greed and indecisiveness in this case takes over amongst other qualities, not being satisfied with one sex that they would need both. Whether or not they like one sex over the next, their appetite is raging that they need it, want it, desire it, crave it, dream about it, anticipate it, honor it and most of all do anything to get it.

Now some are attracted to both sexes equally and then there are others that are attracted to the person, not caring whether it's male or female. Are they greedy, indecisive, confused, spiritually lost, or are they just loving thy neighbor. Now there's others, you know who you are, that past judgment on those bi-sexual women that are dating men and women, bisexual women that are kissing both men and women, bi-sexual women that are performing oral sex on men and women. If you ask any of these women if they had to choose, it would be the woman, hands down.

Chapter 2

A Lady in the Street, but a Freak in the Sheets
(The Bi-Sexual Woman-Shea's Story)

Here I am in a store, browsing, which I don't normally shop in this store but I do see something that is interesting. I move closer for a better look and it looks like it will fit me, just the size I like, and the color is fine as well. Now all I need to do is go try it on and see how it feels against my body. (*In due time, in due time*) So I walk towards what peaked my interest, it is her, I want to see if her conversation is as appealing as her body language.

There she stands with her co-worker and they are both asking me questions about what I do for a living, where do I stay, where or if I hang out etc. by the end of my answers, I was saving both of their numbers in my phone. Shea was the one that peaked my interest when I first walked in. The one on the rack, in the window, on display, which I never pay attention to the display item but hey, I feel like having a new scarf around my neck. Shea was apparently too nervous to call first so me being me I made the first move to contact her, which was about a week after I saved her number. Her voice was so soft and nurturing. I listened to her talk about men and that she wasn't and didn't want to date them anymore because of all the men in her past put her through hell. I couldn't really relate because I have only been with women my whole life. One of many of our important conversations was getting HIV/STD test. So now that we got that out of the way let's get naked! (*No I'm kidding, just kidding!*)

I come off real big and bad, aggressive out the gate but I'm really laid back slow to move and that's what Shea saw. I wasn't aggressive with her trying to get her in bed, well the main reason was that I wanted to make sure that she still wasn't doing dudes. That is a real negative for me (*no licky licky if you're getting dicky dicky*). I didn't even kiss Shea until about a month into our relationship. How shocked she was. I was just taking my time plus I wanted the anticipation to boil. I knew her lips were as soft as

21

they looked. After that first kiss that Shea and I shared, she had already claimed her side of the bed "closest to the door". I knew Shea was a keeper when she comforted me through the night. She whispered sweet words that allowed me to fall deeper into her cuddly embrace.

Did I feel Shea was completely finished dating dudes? No. Why you ask? Because Shea is already in the closet, her family and friends don't know nor do they suspect a thing. Shea would always say that her mom would kill her if she knew that she was dating a woman. Now she acted straight when she was out and about or at work with friends and co-workers. Meaning she still acted interested in guys.

Shea would wake up much earlier than me the following morning dragging from a lack of sleep from the previous nightly games that we played. Shea was thick like I like, that alone turned me on. The way she smelled invited me closer, the way she squirmed and moved invited me inside her. The way she moaned and sucked her bottom lip the wetter my lips became. The more my stamina grew,the ecstasy within her kept building and building and building. (*Until mm mm mm kiss kiss night night*).

Chapter 2

A Lady in the Street, but a Freak in the Sheets
(The Bi-Sexual Woman-Mesha's Story)

Mesha and I were introduced through my business partner, friend, and fellow hustler. I was a hustler and he was a hustler and low and behold she was a hustler. Danny and I hustled dope, Mesha hustled sex. I sold drugs to the community; Mesha sold ___ to the community. I sold drugs to the rich, Mesha sold ___ to the rich, I sold drugs to the educated, Mesha sold ___ to the educated. I sold drugs to the married Mesha sold ___ to the married. I sold drugs to mothers, Mesha sold ___ to fathers. I sold a high, an illusion, a roller coaster ride that they could stay on as long as the price was right. Mesha sold a dream, fantasy, an erection that they could keep as long as the price was right. We were alike in so many ways that we didn't realize, she thought I was the biggest playa, I thought she was the biggest freak. She knew I grabbed everyone's attention when I walked in a room. I knew she grabbed every mans ____ when they walked through the door. Mesha and I spent a great deal of time together, at work, at her place of business, as well as her private abode. I thought and knew that I was all Mesha needed and wanted even though I was already in a great relationship. The adventures that Mesha and I had were personal, emotional, and physical. Mesha's adventures with men were sexual, entertaining some would say full of sin. So as that continued I simply said THE END.

Time passed I missed her, I missed seeing her when she first woke up, I missed her whining about being hungry and asking for waffle house (*Patti melt*) to be exact. I missed the arguments that we would have because I couldn't stay over night. Our relationship began to move, alter, and grow. We moved forward with our friendship. I spent and made more time within and around our relationship. She altered her career, she changed what I wasn't comfortable with her doing, we grew to compromise more, we grew to be more sensitive to one another needs, we grew to appreciate what we had and that was EACH OTHER.

Chapter 2

A Lady in the Street, but a Freak in the Sheets
(The Bi-Sexual Woman-Venus's Story)

Now everybody categorizes the word freak in manners all their own. Some mouths start to water, when you mention he/she is a freak then others snarl and curl their noses at the not so pure manner in activity. Now I on the other hand have always appreciated the flexibility of the female body as well as the creativity a freak possesses. Low and behold did I not know that this day, this freak, this woman would lock her eyes on me. I must admit the shyness that rolled off her tongue, her non-aggressive demeanor when she asked, "are you seeing anyone". I replied, "no" while walking back from being alone with her away from the party that my friend was having. She then asked for my number, I so freely gave her my number. We laughed at her state of shyness, talked about our next encounter, danced to the beat of our feet. I would ask if she needed anything to drink or eat or if I could get her anything. She didn't know it, but I was a caterer by nature, (*so I stepped in as the host for my friend*) so she was in for a real treat. I noticed that she was getting restless, so she let me know that she was about to leave even though the party wasn't quite over with yet, so I proceeded to walk her to her car, which is a sign letting her know that I'm interested even though words aren't coming to fast out of my mouth but this two piece bathing suit of mine sho' is saying a lot.

We talked a great deal over the phone, our conversations were always consistent. We talked about the reasons why she dates guys and women, she explained to me the differences and the likes. She states (*it's not so much of the gender but the person themselves.*) We spoke over the phone more than we saw one another because we lived an hour away from each other. I traveled with clothes and toiletries, well not many clothes. She also traveled to me to spend the night. Did the traveling get old or overwhelming? No. We really enjoyed each other's company. We weren't seeing anyone else at the time. I was single and she was single, so we were able to concentrate on us without any distractions. Venus was older which was great because I loved and preferred older women. She was about seven years my senior.

We meshed spiritually; we expressed our love for God and how we wanted to be pleasing in His eyes. Our dinner dates, whether she cooked at her house or we went out to eat were one on one. We flirted, oh how we flirted with one another in the restaurant at the dinner table, in front of the waiter, around the spectators. Did we mine? Not really. We couldn't wait to leave. Dinner and a movie at the house, well, me in my short see through gown canceled out the typical dinner and a movie. I've always wanted to be dinner and I am always ready for action. Did we have action? Action is an understatement. I wanted her bad, just as bad as she wanted me. I knew where to lick, that made her beg for more. I knew what to caress that made her body do things it's never done. I knew what to say, how to act, and how to treat her that made her want to be mine.

Was she ever really mine?

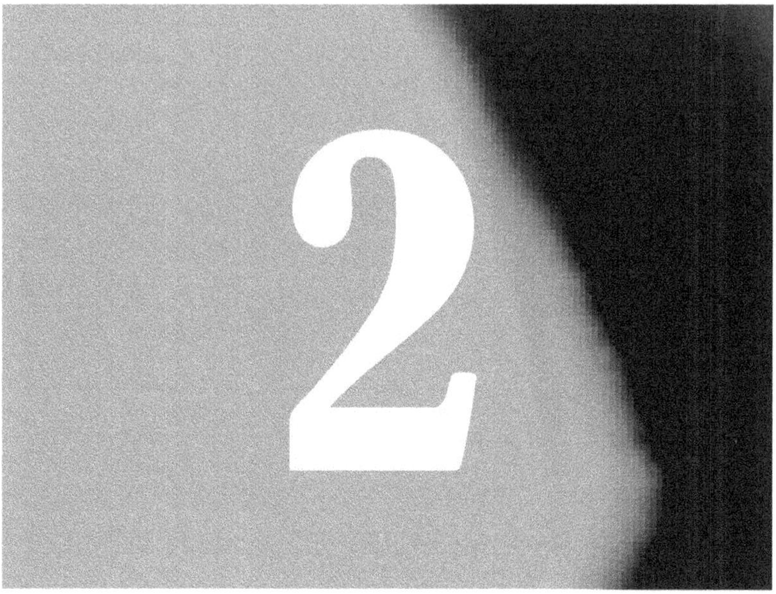
2

A Lady in the Street, but a Freak in the Sheets

The Bi-Sexual Woman

Questions and Answers

Explain sex with a man?
Sex with a man is enjoyable if he loves you, or if he knows what he is doing. If this is the case then it feels wonderful and right if this is not the case it feels like an intrusion.

Explain sex with a woman?
Sex with a woman is also enjoyable if she knows what she is doing however even if she loves me I would need her to know what she was doing as oppose to a man, for me there has to be relational connection or emotional connection and I personally enjoy the build of excitement before having sex almost as much as the act itself.

Favorite female body part?
Legs.

Favorite male body part?
Chest.

What about men you don't like?
His inability to understand me.

What about women you don't like?
Her sharp words during a bad attitude.

What is your greatest pleasure from a woman?
Warmth and affection

What is Bi-Sexuality?
Bi-Sexuality is when I love both male and female equally or not. I may

lean towards one over the other. There are certain things I love and like from a man and there are certain things I love and like from a woman. Certain things only a man can give and certain things only a woman can give.

Are you openly expressive in front of others with loving them both?
It depends on the situation. When I'm around family and friends I show them the side they wanna see. Some family want to see the straight side, some family don't care. When I'm around my friends that date the same sex that's how I act. And then sometimes if I feel like having my girlfriend and my boyfriend there at the same time that's what I do too.

28

It's Nothing Like The First Time
(The Bi-Curious Woman)

Chapter 3

There's Nothing Like the First Time
(The Bi-Curious Woman)

Curiosity killed the cat, which is an old saying but curiosity wants to lick the cat, which is relevant to this chapter.

Have women thought about being with women intimately?
Yes, No, I'll never tell.

This chapter is about those curious women that finally muscled enough courage to take the plunge of being intimate with a woman.
Can a woman be intimate with a woman once and stop?
Is a woman gay/bi-sexual if she sleeps with a woman once?
What considers a woman to be gay/bi-sexual/curious? What is the BIG DEAL about being with another woman-this question posed by all the nosey people that express to you that it's just a phase that you're going through. Now not all curious women stay curious, some say, "what the heck, I'm going in", literally. *(They really mean literally)*. Then there are those other curious women that will sit around wondering how good it will feel to cuddle ever so romantically with another woman. Live your life or live the life your family and friends want you to have.

Chapter 3

There's Nothing Like the First Time
(The Bi Curious Woman-Tasha's Story)

Was it the fact that we worked together, was it my conversation, was it my convertible, was it the Hershey kisses that I left on her desk or was it my subtle inviting wink that drew her closer or maybe the fact that I already had a woman was intriguing enough. She didn't mind until…the more we saw each other at work, the more we wanted to see each other outside of work. The more Hershey's kisses I put on her desk at work the more, she anticipated our first kiss.

The more her family and friends disagreed with the fact that I already had a woman, the more they grew to like me and the more she knew I liked her. The more frustration they showed over our age difference, the more age didn't matter. My job, not the job I was working where I first laid eyes on her, but my real occupation which was law breaking, dangerous, up and down, back and forth, made her feel like she was dating someone who lived on the edge. My focus was to make her feel and know that she was the most important thing, that second, that moment, that day she was in my presence. Even though I had a girlfriend at home, I was able to spend quality time with her, we went shopping together buying clothes that we weren't going to have on for too much longer anyhow.

We grocery shopped for food that we used to nibble off one another and play I'll taste you and you'll taste me adult games. We cuddled to a great movie at her house on the couch. We role-played during sex (*she was the boy, I was the girl*) at her house in the dark, in the living room, alone. I don't believe that there was an inch off her freckled body that I didn't taste. Our late night duck feedings at the park led to horn blows, foggy windows, lean seats, leg cramps, wet cats, moist lips, sweaty palms, teary eyes. Yes, teary eyes we cried almost every time we made love. The passion that came with our love sessions doesn't just happen with everyone you are with.

Why her? I'm not sure but one thing that I am sure of is that she reeked sex. We expressed our love for one another naked and embraced in the rain, on the patio, on a blanket, under a blanket totally involved with nothing or no one else but each other.

Now that she has satisfied her curiosity amongst other things. Can she stop the attraction, those deep, strong feelings that take over her mind when I'm around and when I'm not around? What about those sexual urges, desires, and needs that I continue to meet. Can she say no? Is she just experimenting? If I was no good would her decision be easier? Being curious to try something once is one thing but wanting to altar your whole life is another.

There's Nothing Like the First Time

The Bi-Curious Woman

Question and Answers

What turns you on about women?
Her smile.

Are you infatuated with women?
Only one.

Does she know?
Yes, she's cocky enough to know.

Do you think you could be in a relationship with a woman?
Yes. I think I could if it was a committed relationship.

Could you be with only women or would you still have to be with guys too?
I don't know I'm not sure.

How long have you been curious about the same sex?
Since probably my late teens being close to others who live the lifestyle.

Do you fantasize about women?
All day and all night.

How did you get to the point that you knew you were curious?
The more I see two women holding hands, the more my boyfriend gets on my nerves and doesn't please me sexually and the more the church speaks against the more curious I become.

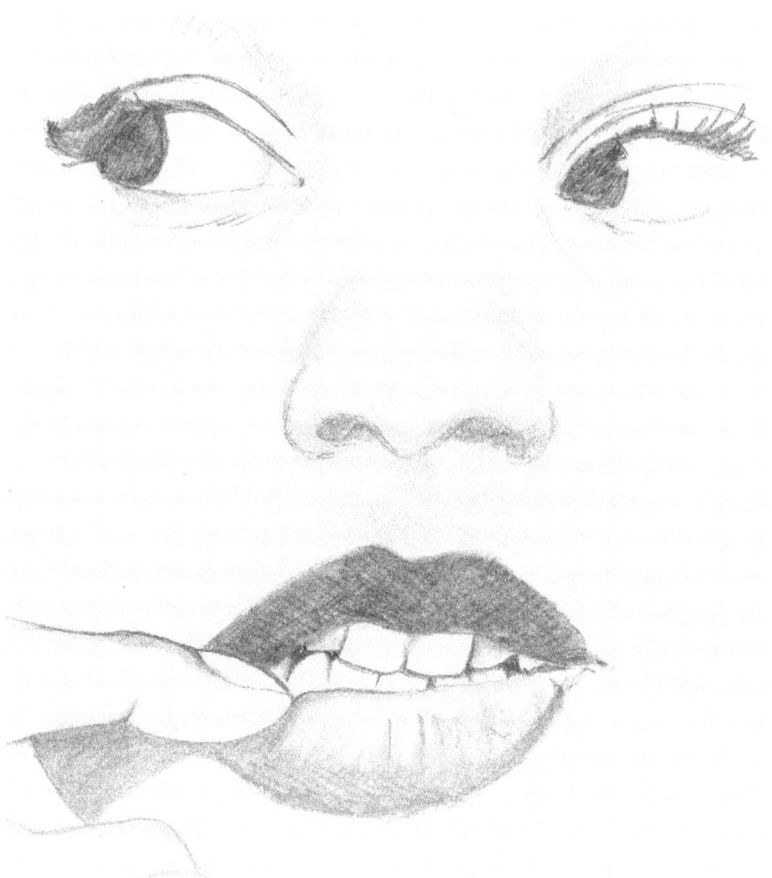

Mind Games
(The Confused Woman)

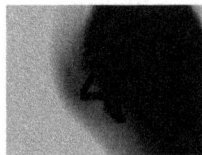

Chapter 4

Mind Games
(The Confused Female)

Peer pressure, T.V., magazines, fitting in, is what we all strive for at the end of the day but these women want to fit in on every angle on the board. One minute they're all in love with the woman, next minute they hate all women. They play straight in and around their straight friends and family then they play gay around the lesbian, they go to all the gay clubs, gay parties, and gay functions. They'll kiss, caress a woman but not in public. They'll let a woman suck on their breast; they may or may not suck back. They'll allow the woman to perform oral sex on them but may or may not perform back.

Majority of this type of women don't do much of anything sexually. Are you yourself a confused woman? Do you have inner thoughts about being with a woman that you try to suppress your desires for the same sex that you haven't/couldn't tell a soul? Who would you tell? Who could you trust? What would your family think? Would they accept you dating a woman? Or are they so against you dating a woman that they would rather accept the fact that you were dating a man that was no good for you? When did these desires for a woman surface? Do you think you could be in a serious relationship with a woman, if your family and friends accepted the life style? Can you classify a confused woman heterosexual, bi-sexual, or lesbian? If you have ever dealt with a confused woman it is no fun, well maybe some parts are fun but if you are looking for settling down, being in a long term committed relationship, that chic is not the one. Why? Because she will never commit to you nor *the lifestyle 100 percent. She'll always have one foot in the door and one foot out the door sorta speak. You'll never be introduced to family as her lover and that's even if you meet any of her family. Lunches with co-workers, doubt it.*

Dinner with the neighbors, maybe. She wants to fit in with society, wife, husband, two kids, a dog, white picket fence, but have you as the best friend sleeping in the guest room. Does the confused woman love the sex from a woman, but of course the sex is ranked #1 on her list.

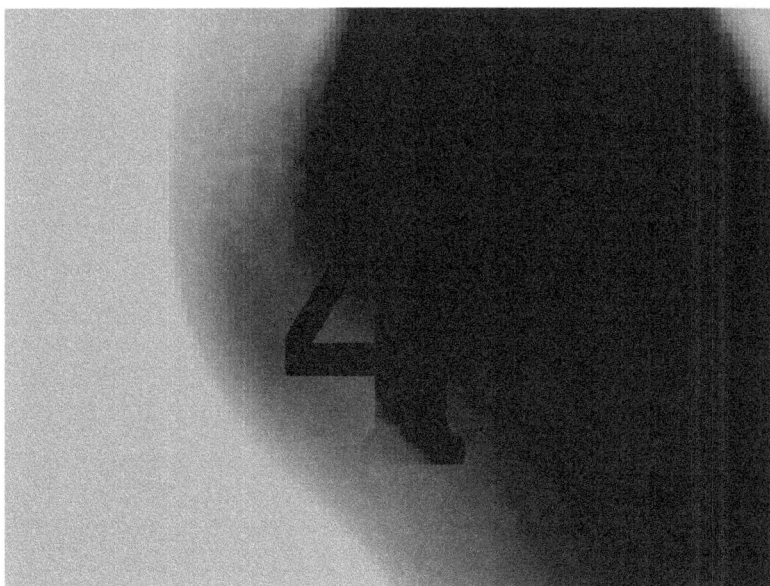

Mind Games

The Confused Female

Questions and Answers

Why women?
Why not? They are caring, gentle, and sexy. There are just so many things that I can address. People are just sexual beings and that's how I see them.

Does family, society, church and friends confuse you?
Yes, but in the end it didn't, I talked to God about it. I talked to my kids about it. Knowing that they are OK with it, I spent many days praying and crying about it. But in the end it's what is important to me. And I know my true friends will stick by me.

If you're somewhere sitting at the park and a male and female both asked you for your number which one will you be more excited to hear from? *The woman of course because I want to satisfy my curiosity.*

Could you be in a committed relationship?
I'm willing to try, I'm excited to see what's behind door number 2.

Speak Now, Or Forever Hold Your Peace
(The Married Woman)

5

Chapter 5

Speak Now or Forever Hold Your Peace
(The Married Woman)

The married women don't seem to think that *(eating ain't cheating)*, I'm here to tell you that you are wrong. Eating is cheating. Maybe they have always thought about being with a woman before and after marriage. I must say if a woman gets involved with a woman, married or not and she likes the experience, which is a huge probability that she will, never leave that woman alone. A woman can't compete with a man and a man can't compete with a woman. How many married woman out there have cheated on their husbands with a woman, their best friends from school, their co-worker that's aggressive but cute, their boyfriends sister that tells her he isn't any good, their sisters girlfriend that thinks she's the cuter one and wants to turn her out anyway. How long do you married women think that you can get away with this cheating? Married women cheat on their husbands, maybe because their husbands are not satisfying them as much or not at all. Did you know that there is a large number of women, heterosexual and bi-sexual, that have never had an orgasm but guess when they do, yep you guessed it, when they are intimate with a woman. You have some married couples that advocate third party sex or three's a charm. Will married women leave their husband for their woman, *it has been done over and over.*

Chapter 5

Speak Now Or Forever Hold Your Peace
(The Married Woman-Leslie's Story)

It wasn't the typical meet and greet in a public setting. It wasn't through mutual friends that we shared. We didn't bump carts in the grocery store line. We weren't standing patiently in the post office line to buy stamps. Our eyes didn't meet across the busy restaurant. We weren't sitting on the same pew praising God together. Our children were not in the same class/school. We weren't stalled at the same red light at the same exact time. We weren't neighbors in the same small community. Our pets didn't run up to each other at the park in the scorching heat.

You want to know where, you ready? Okay I'll tell you.

We met through a reliable source, she has a business, I have a business, so apparently my business intrigued her enough to contact me to know more about my business, my life, my dealings, my struggles, my past, my future. Do know that we corresponded a bit through email, why email and not over the phone? You wonder? Well I gave her my number to contact me so we can go over any and all questions pertaining to my life and past situations but she states through email that she is a boring conversationalist, I surely disagreed and waited patiently until that unknown number would scroll across my screen.

I would have never imagined how one conversation with a woman that I have only seen through photograph and spoke through email, while she states she hadn't thought anything about her conversation was interesting but wasn't I in for a real treat. Our first conversation seemed endless, it was so refreshing, positive, and uplifting.
I was so giddy giddy inside I felt like I was back in high school sucking on a cherry blow pop pacing the floor grinning from ear to ear. We talked for hours even though I was at work. Our conversation was strictly business and it stayed business/professional for some time. Did our conversation start to shift from business/professional to something else? Yes. Something

new, great and consistent.

I knew and felt early on in our conversations how kind and genuine she was, how she didn't push me to talk or express my past or present feelings. Her concern for me melted the layers of unconcern that I have felt in my past.

Did I know she was married? Yes. Have I ever been with a married woman before? Yes. Did that bother me? The overwhelming amount of patience and care blocked any concerns or thoughts I had about her being married...(*to a man that is*) I felt compatible with her, she felt complete with me. She gave me butterflies each and every time I saw her. I nurtured every word that rolled off her tongue, to every hair on her body. Did I feel like I was second? No, because from the time the sun rose until I barely heard traffic on the street, we were on the phone planning our next weekend get away and when the two of us got away together it was as if she wasn't married.

We spent the weekends in bed. We talked in bed about how much we missed one another from our last visit. We watched movies in bed from love stories to x-rated DVD movies, we ate in bed, OH how we ate! We feasted on each other's supple skin until we fell asleep waking up embraced like we just said I DO the night before. Do I have any regrets being with her? *No.*

Chapter 5

Speak Now or Forever Hold Your Peace
(The Married Woman-Claire's Story)

We shared something much more than the average typical everyday, fly by night qualities that we mainly have for one another. We shared the love of one individual that was married with children and the other not married but in a committed relationship. Now you ask was she happily married? What is the true/real definition of happily married? Was I true to my committed relationship? I never missed a beat, on letting and making sure that my lover knew and felt how committed I was and how valuable she meant to me. Claire and I shared realness growing in the way that old couples start out and are still married today, 40 years strong, with stories that could/would influence any and every individual to reconnect with their better half.

We were introduced to one another through a mutual acquaintance not knowing whether we would even like one another other or not but I guess that's the whole rush, the not knowing.

Our conversations started off pretty typical, we started talking about our families, who we were close to and who really didn't care to much about us, hey, you have these in every family. So along with that we had a few other things in common as well, like music, we both absolutely love old school music that we would sit up on the phone until the wee hours of the morning listening to music and playing name that tune. Where was her husband you ask? Not sure, maybe sleep or at work. Where was my girlfriend, oh she was sleep, she knew and was home the time Claire and I were talking and playing on the phone but mainly it was when my girl had already went to sleep. Did Claire and I see one another even though she had a husband and I had a girlfriend? Yes. I would travel to where she was, to visit, to hang out and spend some one on one time together. We weren't able to spend a great deal of time with one another because we didn't live in the same state but we did make up for it over the phone every time we talked, our desire for one another increased. How was it when we were together you ask? We were like two goofy puppets that joked, played, laughed every chance we got, we both have outgoing personalities. Were/when were we intimate? Yes. When? When we were alone in her house, no kids, no husband, at night when the kids were sleep and her husband was working. There is an old saying that says the mouse will play when the cat is away.

She was willing and ready to do what she had never done and she wanted to be a big girl finally then that's when I submitted to her. I'm usually the aggressor but I have no problem being passive and submissive every now and then. Did I have any regrets sleeping with a married woman? No. Did she and I sleeping together affect the friendship between her husband and I? No, he never suspected a thing, nor did she and I change the way we acted in front of one another. We were able to maintain that platonic/no affection in front of her husband, children, and friends. Sneaking around from family/friends was not what we were about. We were about enjoying each day that we had together.

Speak Now Or Forever Hold Your Peace

The Married Woman

Questions and Answers

Can you be married to a woman?
Yes, of the two relationships that I was in I felt like I could.

Why haven't you divorced your husband?
I am afraid to do that, because I know I was wrong to have ever stepped outside of my marriage.

Are you sleeping with your husband and a woman?
Yes I want to satisfy my husband's needs and I wanted to satisfy my own desires of being with a woman.

Has there ever been a threesome, and have you ever thought about it?
No and No.

Will you leave your husband for her?
Sometimes I felt like I would have but then reality settles in and God pulls me back.

Does she know that you are married and does it bother her?
Yes and Yes.

Does your husband approve?
He doesn't know.

What would your family think?
I don't know.

What is your advice to other married women?
Stay monogamous; find a way to stay true.

Were you with women before you got married?

No because I never had the courage to approach women and was never in an area that a woman would approach me, and even if I was and another woman did approach me I probably would not know I was being approached.

What is your greatest pleasure?

Holding her in my arms, or being held in her arms.

Will you ever stop?

Yes because she and I both made a decision to stop and I know that I don't want to be a part of something that I am ashamed of or that makes her ashamed. I have no problem explaining to others but I would be ashamed to tell my child that I am living a dishonest life.

When you dated women were you open in public?

No, I let some people know. I was not comfortable enough to let everyone know.

Through Thick & Thin (The Best Friend)

Chapter 6

Through Thick and Thin
(The Best Friend)

I'll do anything for you, you'll do anything for me, shake on it, pinky promise, friends to the end, I swear, cross my heart hope to die stick a needle in my eye, I'll cover for you, my lips are sealed, quiet mouse, *shhhh*, don't worry, I got your back, sisters for life, best friends forever, nothing but death can keep me from her.

These are some of the phrases that we recognize between two best friends. Friends share everything, jokes, laughter, clothes, money, advice, secrets/trust, responsibility, household duties, financial decisions, childcare, cooking, cleaning, sharing of each other self, space, time, mood swings, affections, compassion and of course sexual needs.

This relationship works and thrives in so many areas because you have two well-rounded, well-liked, well-known women that may or may not have grown up together. May or may not have known each other for numerous of years but have built a bond, foundation of trust, pureness, wholesomeness, and dedication. They have found themselves, who they want to be, who they want to be with, who they have become, why did it take me so long to get here, to find you, to be happy, to feel loved, to feel complete said one woman.

Chapter 6

Through Thick and Thin
(The Best Friend-Tab's Story)

Like others Tab and I started off co-workers, after each clock-in, after each lunch break, after each night shift we grew above and beyond your average best friend. It had gotten to the point where us working together just wasn't cutting it. It was just pacifying us for the BIG PICTURE. We passed notes as best friends do during work, at the same time, with the same pen, with the same BF 4 EVER logo at the bottom. Typical bf stuff. We hung out all night, after work talking, drifting on each other's sentences, hanging on to each other's words, talking about what you ask? Life, love, family, children, school, work, career, clothes, cars, food, etc. you name it we talked about it and laughed about it.

We enjoyed sitting close to one another on the hood of her car, she looking up at the stars, I'm looking at her wondering what do I have to do to get closer to her heart, mind, and her body. We took our best friend status to a whole 'nother level. We moved in together, shared furniture, dishes and even the same bath towel from time to time. I was patient but I knew that I wanted to be more than just best friends. I was waiting for just that right moment to say "can I have you?" "Can I do what you need me to do, can I be your ultimate lover, *and I will have you climaxing in your sleep.*

Do we get tired of one another? No. Do we share things like clothes? No we are not the same size. Who cooks? Me mainly. Who Cleans? Me mainly. Who pays when we go out? That would be her. Who drives? Who ever feels like it at the time. Who holds the door open? That would be her. Who pays the bills? She holds that title. Who makes decisions on what to do and where to go? Both of us. Who's more aggressive in bed? Me. Is there a benefit in being best friends first? But of course, you can't build anything off of sex in the first place. Friendship takes time to cultivate and nurture. Communication is the godfather of all qualities; you don't know what your mate likes to do coming home from work if you don't communicate. You don't know how your mate likes to be handled in bed

53

unless you don' t communicate etc. etc. etc. that wasn't an issue for Tab and I because that's all we did was communicate.

First we were best friends, talking about our likes, dislikes, and wants, needs and desires. Then we became roommates talking about bills, neighbors, and the good old mailman running late again. Now we are lovers talking about, well we weren't doing too much talking *"cat got our tongues"*.

Chapter 6

Through Thick and Thin
(The Best Friend-G's Story)

I'll start off by saying G was the kind of best friend that you see perceived on a good old tearjerker movie. G was that best friend that scrolled across your TV set every Wednesday night on your favorite family sit com. G was that best friend in one of those love me, buy me, commercials. G was the best friend that everyone strives to become but just didn't have it within.

G helped me when I didn't think I needed help. G allowed me to feel extremely comfortable with her and comfortable within my own skin. Early on in our friendship she never pushed me to open up emotionally, she knew that I was kind of quiet. So she focused on being my best friend being there those times when I needed her just to be in the same room and being there those times I needed her just to hold me.

G never judged me for what I did or what I didn't do. The way she formed her words to tell me how special I was ministered to my soul the way her eyes met mine when she expressed the unconditional amount of love that she shares for me. The deeper our bond had gotten the more I realized I couldn't be away from her at any given time.

The desires I had for my best friend was strong and getting stronger. We had found ourselves not just cuddling, watching a good movie but holding hands, waiting for the other one to lean in for that first kiss. Was this kiss with my best friend suppose to feel so good and so right? Do I feel guilty because we were best friends and best friends don't kiss and hold hands? No, I want to do it again and again. Who else better to kiss than the one that I trust and the one I'm most comfortable with.

That kiss from G, my best friend leads me to watching her dress and bathe, memorizing each birth mark along side her back. Caressing her face with my face as she slept wishing, hoping, heart pounding so hard from the unknown, wanting her to wake up and make love to me like in my dreams, wanting to drown myself in those three little words "I love you" as she whispers in my ear in between each ear lobe nibble. Every time I graze my bottom lip over her motionless lips she moves a little. Should I wake my best friend up and say *make love to me* or should I just let her sleep and I continue to dream of that magic happening. My lips touch hers in a good night kiss and I go to bed.

I'm dreaming again and this time it feels like I'm awake or like its really happening but my eyes are closed. I'm being caressed and fondled in every which way. I open one eye, oh how sweet I can't believe it. I open the other eye, its my best friend she must have read all of my signals. She whispers, "I've been wanting you", "I say you can have me", she makes love to my mind, heart and soul. I never felt so good, I never felt so refreshed, relieved. I felt like it was my very first time. G made me feel like nothing else mattered at that moment, just her and I. I'm in love with my BEST FRIEND.

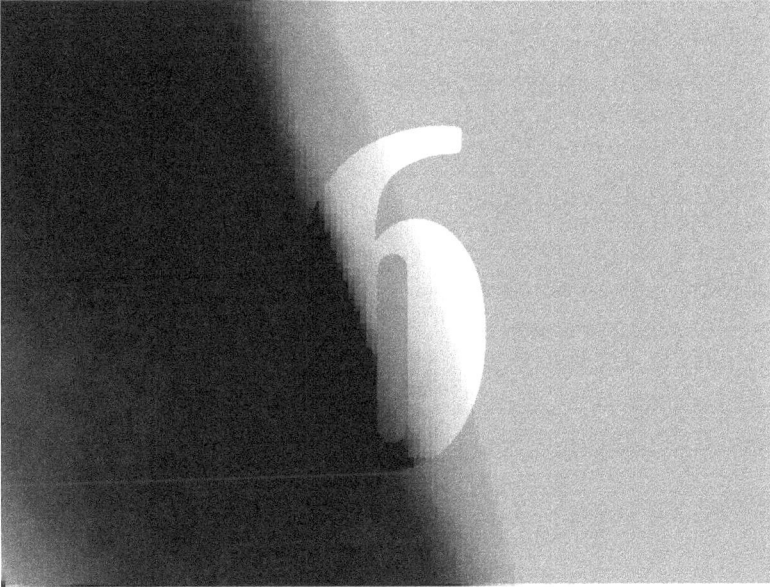

Through Thick and Thin

The Best Friend

Question and Answers

Do you always sleep with your best friend?
No however the ones I have been with just happened to be my bff.

Can you go back to just being friends after being lovers?
In some cases yes and some cases no, but in my case I have not lost any friends.

How do you view your friendship now?
I view my most recent friendship with the same deep love and hope to stay friends for eternity.

Did family friends and co-workers ever suspect or insinuate that you guys were closer than normal?
People always seem to think what they want, maybe they are envious or jealous and instead of trying to understand that we are close they make assumptions...in some cases its true.

How do best friends turn into lovers?
The same way any relationship occurs it just happens, so many times people put a limit on being in love. Being in love with someone isn't just for marriage but for anyone who you feel close enough to hold that much of your heart and for me my best friend. It's just that close.

What happen to the boundaries that best friends shouldn't cross?
Would you ask a male and female who are best friends that end up lovers the same question? I believe boundaries are meant to protect, in the case of a loving relationship there shouldn't be boundaries to withholding love.

Have you and your best friend ever displayed any public?
Yes we have

Let The Truth
Be Told...
(The Real Lesbian Woman)

7

Chapter 7

Let the Truth Be Told
(The Real Lesbian Woman)

Ever since I was a young girl, I gravitated toward little people that look like me. I was expressing my love for them in ways that I really didn't understand. All I knew was that I didn't want to have anything to do with the opposite sex. Did I know or understand why I liked girls and not boys? Yes I knew then at an early age being faced with my greatest fear even today that I was being sexually abused by family members three to be exact Father, Uncle, Brother. I felt like I didn't or wasn't given the choice of what life to lead Heterosexual/Homosexual. I feel I gravitated toward homosexuality because of the men in my family that were suppose to be role models and overseers that molded this lesbian I am.

Am I mad?

I'm mad, hurt, angry, disgusted, bitter, confused, scorned, and damaged. Because of what they did and how they did it.

Am I unhappy because I date women? No. Do I love women? Yes. Am I attracted to women? Yes. Am I attracted to men? No. Do I kiss Women? Yes. Do I make love to women? Yes. Can I see myself being intimate with a man? No. I love everything about a woman, the sway in her step, the sweetness of her tone, the moistness of her lips, the wetness of her cat, the deepness of her eyes, the texture of her hair, the small of her back, the roller coaster motions of her body, the softness of her hands, the smoothness of her tongue, the safe secure embrace of her arms, the sassy mood swings, the mature independence, the take charge attitude.
I did any and every thing there was and is to do with a woman sexually. I made love with everything I did from waking them up by caressing up and down their inner thigh with my oh so moist tongue, to them coming outside and seeing roses all over their car before going to work, to preparing their dinner, running their bath, in turn I'm the wash cloth, to getting their clothes out for the week, to undressing them in 2.2 seconds,

my mouth whispered I love you in their ear, my eyes read I want only you, my mouth would caress every single inch of their body, while my fingers/hands tamed every quiver/squirm of flesh, my legs wrapped around hers so tight to spread them even further than she imagined they could spread. My arms clenching her ever so closer, so she could feel the intense passion that I had for her.

I only want to straddle a woman,
I only want a woman to sit on my face.

I am the real lesbian woman.

Let the Truth Be Told

The Real Lesbian Woman

Question and Answers

What made you a lesbian?
I don't think I had a choice whether I lived my life as a lesbian or as a heterosexual woman. Those men that violated me moved on and lived their life like nothing ever happened, like they did no wrong, like they didn't just wreck the rest of my life. Like me I was abused/violated but not all lesbians today have been abused and violated. Every lesbian has a different background, story, ethnicity, religion and upbringing. We can't compare any two stories the same.

How has society viewed you?
Society, society, society, when is the society, the world, the church, the government ever quiet and just mind their own business. I'm sick of people telling me what somebody said, what they believe, what groups write about, what is portrayed across the T.V. screen. What does Shawna FEEL?

What is your greatest pleasure?
Security. I've never had security in my life until I started dating women.

Why can't a beautiful woman find room for a handsome man?
You tell me.

Do you have ill feelings toward the men that done you wrong?
But of course.

Were you sexually abused/raped?
Yes.

What is your sexual gratification from being with a woman?

65

The intensity of emotions and the softness of her embrace.

What is the emotional attachment?
Everything that a woman says, does, how she walks, her demeanor the way she carries herself, her outlook on life, love, friendship and parenting. The way a woman smells, the softness of her hands, feet, curvature of her thighs, hips, small of her back, roundness of her buttocks, the sound of her voice, the wind in her hair, the sensitivity, the compassion, the consistency, the ability to nurture, the I can fix it attitude...what is there not to love about a woman.

Are they tired of being lied to from the male gender?
Yes.

Do you think and know that you are a sinner?
The bible speaks against it.

Do you think you're going to heaven?
I haven't thought about it.

Do you think its okay for two women to be married?
Yes why not, I think it's beautiful.

Why does a woman get puffed up when a man is trying to holler at her girl?
Maybe some women are intimidated by men.

How do you feel being in public with your woman?
I feel like I'm on top of the world.

Do you feel self-conscience?
No should I?

The choice that you made, are you ready for the ridicule that comes from your children, family, and society?
When my child is old enough to understand and comprehend I will explain

and clarify my lifestyle and position as a mother.

Most men are cool with women that are gay. Why?
Well I think men always have an ulterior motive thinking they can change her or change her back.

Most women are cool with men that are gay. Why?
Because a lot of the gay men are feminine and act like women any way so he's just one of the girls.

Are you happy with what you are doing?
Yes, I feel comfortable and complete.

Was it a choice or by force?
I would have to say force, I don't feel like I had a choice, I feel like the decision or this lifestyle was thrust upon me.

Why do you think you lean towards females than males?
The tragic pain that I felt during my childhood from the male gender.

Compared to a man what does a woman offer you?
A woman will more likely know when to nurture.

Could a man have the same qualities that you see in a woman?
I'm sure, I guess.

When did you find out you were attracted to women?
I knew early on when I was just a child that I gravitated towards people that look just like me, as I grew older well into my teen years that's when it became sexual.

Is it physical or emotional?
BOTH!

Are you open with your lifestyle?
I was never discreet; I have always been open publicly with my sexuality.

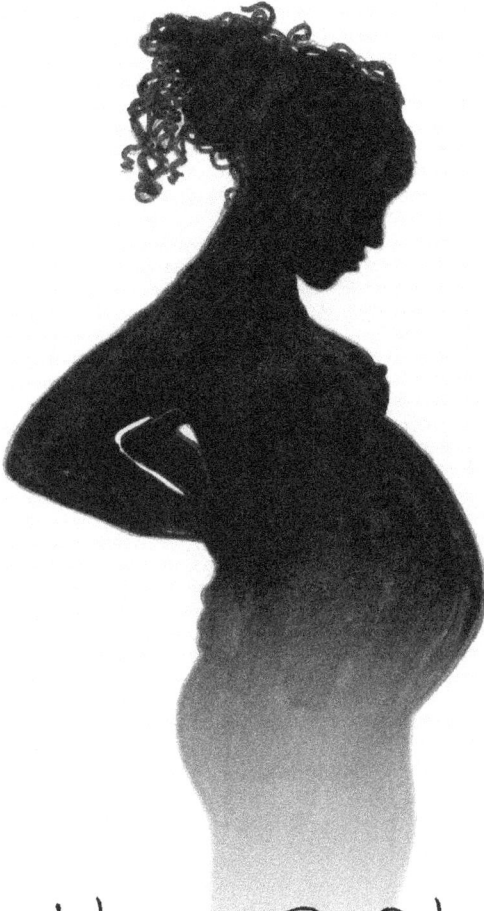

Mother & Child
(The Lesbian Parent)

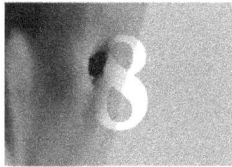

Chapter 8

Mother and Child
(The Lesbian Parent)

Can you be a great mother living a lesbian lifestyle and raise your
children up to be productive God fearing adults? How does society treat,
criticize and look at you for being a lesbian with child?
Some say you shouldn't bear children with the same sex, others say you
shouldn't be allowed to adopt being as the same sex as your partner.

So-called Christians are just disgusted by the facts and gossip about you
when you arrive late to church service. *Oh lets not forget that people that
call themselves Christians are perfect, without fault, without sin.*

Do you have preachers, senators, debaters plus an enormous amount of
organizations rallying against lesbian parents? What does the word of God
say? Does God speak against that same sex relationships can't raise
children? Do the children grow up unbalanced? Do the children face
ridicule? What is unbalanced? Being raised with one parent is unbalanced
enough. All children face ridicule in some point in their childhood,
true/false. Do the children grow up liking, feeling, loving, wanting, and
needing, to be with the same sex? How many heterosexual parents have a
gay/lesbian child?

Yeah I'm talking to you while you have that not so pleasant look on your
face.

Can I relate, yes, said the lesbian parent that is.

I raised my biological nephew as my son while in a lesbian relationship
for years. Should gay/lesbian parents teach their child it's wrong/right to
be gay/lesbian?

I have been in countless lesbian relationships where we both took full responsibility of raising our children or disciplining them, to picking out school clothes for the week, to making sure their church clothes were not wrinkled. We both shared by checking and helping with homework, and setting a designated study time. Together we grocery shopped, only buying the things that the kids loved the most. I cooked, she cooked, and the kids set the table.

Some relationships we ate at the table the majority of the time and then sometimes we ate in the family room. While other times we made sure we were eating in the same room at least. We watched good entertaining movies and family sitcoms with our children, as well as we maintained just what they would entertain their little minds with.

We changed diapers, taught how to drive, and explained how our female on female relationship expressed and true love, feelings and attraction for one another. We've done and did everything a normal heterosexual family could do, (*husband, wife, and kids*) that women on women raising children could do. We've been on vacations to the beach, theme parks, and water parks. Our kids have not been without.

At our family functions, like thanksgiving, where the whole family get together to fellowship, was our lesbian life style, or relationship, or the way that were raising our children, discussed, at the table so casually, like the weather, like sports, of course not. Why not? Probably because our family and friends, the ones that we socialize with on a regular basis have the concept of respect. Respecting ones lifestyle as their own. I as well as countless other lesbians have lived a normal life with women, going to church, tithing together, worshiping together. I've even been taught from them what I didn't know about God and His word. We have taken each other on vacations without the kids because of course we also need our quality alone time. Just as much as any heterosexual couple would. We've experienced long walks on the beach hand in hand, making love by the fire, to good ole' hot and steamy passionate I want you now sex, in the car on the way home. We've kissed openly and embraced in public, as heterosexual couples would do.

Do people throw things? Or get up and leave the establishment where we are? No. I have never been kicked out of a restaurant, screen play, comedy show, bank etc., for loving on my woman in public. Do people stare? But of course they do. Does that bother me? No. I've held my woman's hand, kissed her at every public place you can think of that we have frequented. I have no shame. Now, has every woman I have been with, been as open with their sexuality as me? No.

Our children have grown up to be amazing children, well liked, well groomed, well mannered, respectful, polite, energetic, smart, and talented. I can go on and on but some say that lesbians cant and shouldn't raise or be able to adopt and love children as their own.

Whose to say that the way heterosexual parent raising their children are better and more rewarding than the way lesbians raise their children just because you have two lesbians raising children don't mean that they don't and can't grow up to be productive, law abiding, thoughtful, nurturing citizens.

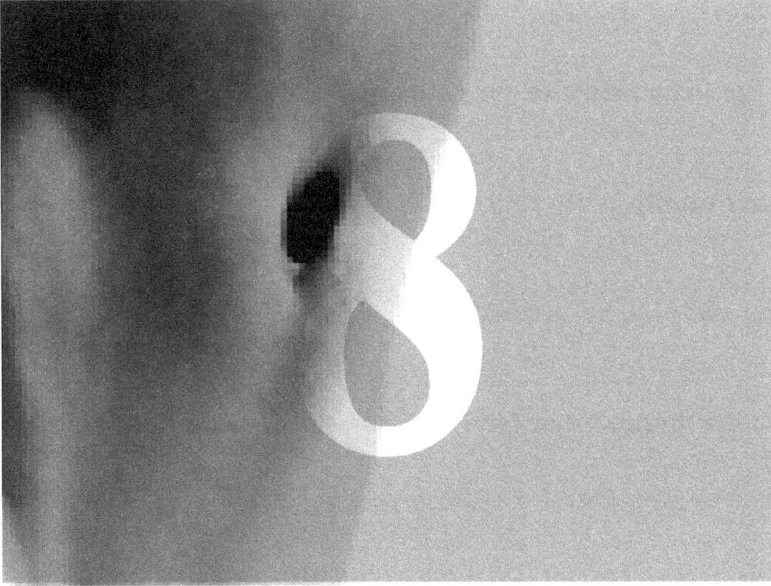

The Lesbian Parent

Mother and Child

Question and Answers

Have you been ridiculed for your lifestyle?
Yes

Has your family ostracized you?
No but there have been discussions and confrontations about it.

Do your children get teased?
Yes.

Do you get threats from family and friends to take your children away?
Yes, but they have only been idle threats my kids are still with me.

What do your children feel about your lifestyle?
They don't confront me about it, they do have questions but this is all they have ever known.

What have you expressed to your children about lesbianism?
What haven't I? I have explained what it is, and just because I am this way doesn't mean they will be. People say negative things but its more than two people having sex. Now that they are getting older the conversations about lesbianism and homosexuality and my lifestyle are becoming more in depth.

Are you open affectionately around your children with your lover?
Yes.

Are you still attracted to men?
Sure men are cute and some are sexy. But I just don't have the desire to be intimate with any of them.

Greatest pleasure from a woman?
The bond that two woman have and share, the sex is good, I also gravitate towards emotional connection.

Are you open with your sexuality?
Yes.

I Just Don't Get It
(The Heterosexual Woman)

Chapter 9

I Just Don't Get It
(The Heterosexual Woman)

"I just don't get it" Is the name of this chapter, now I think there's a small few that don't get it but then I feel it is a large number that do get it, understand it, can relate to it, have dreamed about it, read about it, watched girl on girl movies, sat down and listened to the conversations, snuck and read those articles about those celebrities that are coming out openly about their lesbian lifestyle.

Now don't get me wrong I do believe that there are some true, real heterosexual women out there, I know quite a few. They can't fathom being touched by a woman in an intimate way, in an intimate setting. Real heterosexual women are not curious, they don't ponder over the thought of wondering if this chick can lick the cat better than her dude.

Real heterosexual women are not curious, they don't undress other women with their eyes nor do they sneak a peak at their friends getting dressed. Real heterosexual women are not curious, to know or find out if a dildo feels the same as a real penis. Real heterosexual women are not curious about who is going to pay when they go out because they clearly are not. Real heterosexual women are not curious, THEY JUST DON"T GET IT!

Chapter 9

The Heterosexual Woman

Question and Answers

What do you think about when you see two women together like that?
I don't think anything, what am I suppose to think.

Have you ever thought about being with a woman?
I've been approached but no.

Why do you think women gravitate towards other women?
Probably from something they are missing. I have a couple of friends that are that way because of the molestation they went through.

What confuses you the most about lesbians?
Lesbians feel like all women have had the desire to be with other women- why would they think that? I never yearned a desire to be with a woman.

Do you understand?
To a certain degree some women feel like other women can give them that emotional side that they don't get from a man.

Do you have lesbian friends?
Yes lesbian friends and lesbian family members.

What were you taught about homosexuality?
Nothing against homosexuality but I was taught acceptance in my home life but in the church I was taught that homosexuality and lesbianism was an abomination. I attended that church but the church I worked at, had an inclusive ministry which accepted homosexuality.

Are you disgusted?
No. It is a growing and learning process for me. It was gross to me at the beginning, lesbianism isn't just about the sexual act its more of an emotional attachment just as a woman would have with a man.

Would you be with a woman to please your man?
I don't know I can't say yes or no.

Do you look at lesbians and bisexuals the same?
What's different? This day and time you just don't know.

What do you think about women that do both men and women?
I guess I still love them because I have one in my family. With her she is still searching. I think she/they have high sex drives.

The Male Perspective

10

Chapter 10

<u>The Male Perspective</u>

Do you know the percentage of men that have been with more than one woman at a time? Do you know the percentage of men that want to be with more than one woman at the same time? Do you know the percentage of men that don't have that share my wife, share my girlfriend desire? Why is it that men are so turned on by two women making out? Why is it some or more than some actually make being with two women their dream, desire, passion, and a want? Does that make a man a pervert? Is he a freak? Is his sex drive stronger than the man who does not have a desire to be with two women?

Are wives obligated to fill their husbands desire by sleeping with a woman? Are the men expressing this fantasy to their mate early on? Is it a new thing, trend, fad to have been with two women at the same time. Males some (*and more than some*) understand the female on female relationship because men know that women will give other women what they need. How many women will admit to sleeping with another woman for the satisfaction of her husband?

Are men intimidated by lesbians? Are men intimidated by the gay women that look like dudes? How does a man approach a woman who has a girlfriend? Can a man marry an ex-lesbian and not think or ask her to have a ménage a trois? Can a husband marry an ex-lesbian and have assurance that she won't commit adultery with a woman?

Chapter 10

"The Male Perspective"

Questions and Answers

"Is every man turned on by two women?"

What is it that turns you on about two women?
More or less sanity, double your pleasure, the entertainment value.

How do you approach women with the question?
Start off playful, then if she reciprocates be straightforward.

Are women willing and eager?
Some. That's if the woman asks the other woman.

Do/did they know one another?
Don't have to but it's nice to have some kind of acquaintance.

Are the women doing each other?
Depends on the comfort level of the woman.

Do you do both women?
Yes.

Why have two if only one watches?
Communicate first about what happens, and what don't happen.

Will you want your wife and to be able to try a threesome?
I'm open-minded and if she's open-minded we will discuss it.

Does this give a man bragging rights?
No

Do you approach lesbians?
The feminine ones you can't tell, the masculine women I befriend, I don't try to convert lesbians but most men do.

Foreplay is a lost art that most men have forgotten about.

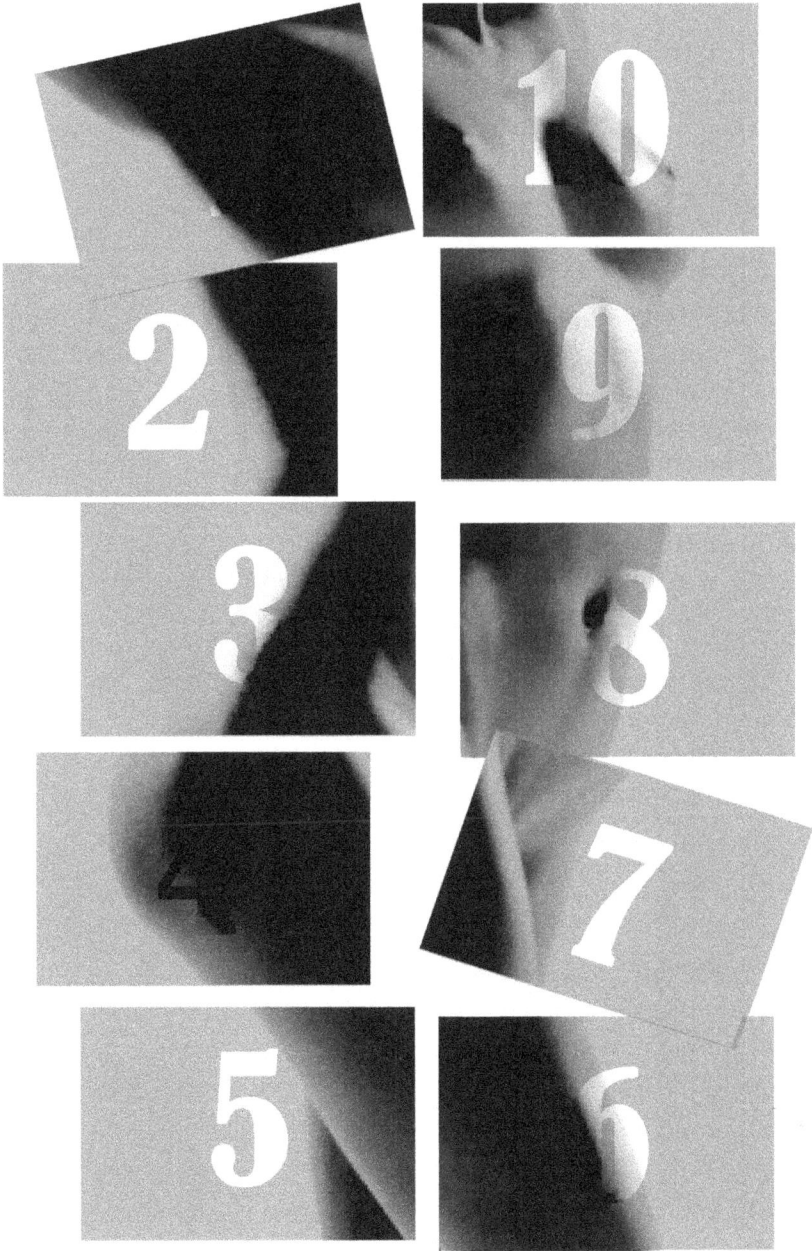

EPILOGUE

Was this book the truth, whole truth and nothing but the truth? Yes. Have I lived a lesbian lifestyle my whole life? Yes. Did I love women? Yes. Did I think and dream of marrying a woman? Yes. Was I open in/out of public with my sexuality? Yes. Am I still breathing, walking, living a lesbian lifestyle? No. Why? I Shawna Monique Harrison have been convicted of the lifestyle. Was it my decision to leave the lesbian lifestyle? No. Whose was it? God's! Would I have ever made that decision? No. Was I confused, hurt, devastated, broken? Yes. And every emotion one individual could feel, I felt. Why me? I repeatedly asked God. He made me tired of feeling the way that I was feeling, fed up with dealing with what I was dealing with. God opened my eyes to see His Word, which showed me my future, my destiny, my purpose, and a woman was nowhere in that equation. He opened my heart to accepting me and accepting my past as though it was and not who I am. I am learning to love me because my Father God wants me to love me. He loves me even when I didn't love me, that I tried so hard not to be here. Did my suicide attempts have anything to do with the lesbian lifestyle? No. The fact that I didn't love me, did that have anything to do with the lesbian lifestyle? No. I feel like God wants something more from me, a new chapter, a new book, a new walk, a new lifestyle, a renewing of my mind. Apparently He sees something in me that I didn't or don't.

To learn more about my childhood, upbringing and life as a whole, please read my first autobiography "MY TRUE SOUL EXPLOITED, APREHENDED, AND BROKEN WITHIN" I as the author tell all as you just read in "LET THE TRUTH BE TOLD" I hold nothing back, from the time that I was six years old until my adulthood, I speak about the sexual abuse I endured from family members, the battle with self mutilation, the abandonment from my parents etc.

I, Shawna the Author take you into my world.

Am I suggesting that you should lead a homosexual lifestyle? No. Am I suggesting that you should leave the homosexual lifestyle? No. Am I saying that marrying a woman knowing that you are a woman is right/wrong? No. Am I saying that sex with a woman is better than with a man? No. I only know women. Am I saying that God don't love you? No. All I will say is that I don't have a heaven or hell to put anyone in, so why would I, why should I and how can I judge you or anyone for that matter. We all have to answer for our own actions. I will say, where ever you are in your life, love yourself and build your relationship with God.

Glossary

-Aggressive Fem - A feminine lesbian with an aggressive demeanor

-Pillow Princess - Lesbian that only receives

-Diesel Dyke - Masculine lesbian

-Carpet Muncher - Lesbians that perform oral sex

-Lipstick - Feminine lesbian

-Bull Dyke - Masculine lesbian

-Lesbo - Short for lesbian

-Stud - Lesbian that dresses and acts like a boy

-Soft Stud (Tweener) - Looks like a girl but dresses like a boy

-Butch - Masculine lesbian

-Bi Sexual - A woman that likes boys and girls

-Brother - This is what gay studs refer to each other as

-Legit - A gay and lesbian immigration task force which is an organization that helps same sex couples with immigration

-Dignity - An organization of gay and lesbian Catholics that work for the acceptance of gays.

-Down Low - whose public identification is straight but who have discreet sex with other women outside of their primary relationship

-Fem - the more feminine woman in the relationship.

-Gaydar - the ability of gays to tell if others are gay even when they are in the closet. The key is eye contact.

-GLB - Gay, Lesbian, Bisexual

-GLBT - Gay, Lesbian, Bisexual, Transgender

RESOURCES

Exodus International
www.exodusinternational.org

Exodus is a non profit, interdenominational christian organization promoting the message of freedom from homosexuality through the power of Jesus Christ.

Joseph Coat Ministries
www.josephcoatministries.com

Is change possible? Joseph Coat Ministries affirms that reorientation of homosexuality/same sex attraction is possible. This is a process that begins with motivation and self determination to change based upon a personal relationship with Jesus Christ.

Cross Ministry
www.crossministry.org

FirstStone Ministry
www.firststone.org

Leading people in the body of Christ to freedom from homosexuality and sexual brokenness through Jesus Christ.

Parents and Friends of Ex Gays
www.pfox.org

PFOX is a national non profit organization that support families, advocates for the ex gay community and educates the public on sexual orientation. Works to eliminate negative perceptions and discrimination against former homosexuals.

LET THE TRUTH BE TOLD
Life of Women on the Down Low

SHAWNA M. HARRISON

To contact the author for more information, to order more books, to book for speaking engagements or to publish your own books, go to her website:

www.shawnaharrison.com

or email her at:
shawna_mytruesoul@yahoo.com

HER TRU SOUL PUBLISHING
www.hertrusoulpublishing.com

www.ingramcontent.com/pod-product-compliance
Lightning Source LLC
Chambersburg PA
CBHW031222090426
42740CB00007B/675